She Watered Her Flowers in the Morning

poems by

Marsha Owens

Finishing Line Press
Georgetown, Kentucky

She Watered Her Flowers in the Morning

Copyright © 2022 by Marsha Owens
ISBN 978-1-64662-998-5 First Edition
All rights reserved under International and Pan-American Copyright Conventions. No part of this book may be reproduced in any manner whatsoever without written permission from the publisher, except in the case of brief quotations embodied in critical articles and reviews.

ACKNOWLEDGMENTS

Grateful acknowledgment is made to the following print and online publications in which these poems originally appeared.

A Wild Word Anthology: "Sometimes Guests Overstay Their Welcome"
NewVerseNews: "Bad Things Happen When Roosters Crow and Dance"
Poets Reading the News: "No Consolation" and "After the Singing"
Rat's Ass Review: "Facebook Seduction in God-Awful Times" and "Divorce"
Rise Up Review: "For Aylan"
Streetlight Magazine: "Some Days"
The Literary Nest: "Ugly Times"

Special thanks to my teachers, Leslie Shiel and Roselyn Elliot, and to my daughter, Tamara Hubbard, and my friends, Margaret McKinnon and Nan Ottenritter, who carefully read through drafts, and to Joanna Lee, founder, River City Poets, who first encouraged me to write again and write some more.

Publisher: Leah Huete de Maines
Editor: Christen Kincaid
Cover Art: Marsha Owens
Author Photo: Tamara Hubbard
Cover Design: Elizabeth Maines McCleavy

Order online: www.finishinglinepress.com
also available on amazon.com

Author inquiries and mail orders:
Finishing Line Press
PO Box 1626
Georgetown, Kentucky 40324
USA

Table of Contents

I.
Some Days 1
For Aylan 2
When the Video Runs on Fast Forward 3
Sometimes Guests Overstay Their Welcome 4
After the Singing 5

II.
Sunday Church on the Deck 9
NYC Sidewalk 10
Bad Things Happen When Roosters Crow and Dance 11
FB Seduction in God-awful Times 12
No Consolation 13
I Can Only Do Today 14
Ugly Times 15
Pete 16
You Never Forget Your Shooting 17
A Girl Story, circa 1960 18
Women in the Shadows 19
Judge Stepford 20
Who are the Dead 21

III.
Divorce 25
Can a Day be Too Pretty 26
Exhale 27
She Watered Her Flowers in the Morning 28
My Tree 29

I.

*Give sorrow words; the grief that does not speak
Knits up the o'er wrought heart and bids it break.*
   —William Shakespeare

Some Days
> *for my mother*

when the horizon dips
into darkness unsure about dawn,
I touch the faded photo, your face
still wears a wisp of pink, blurred
now by brushed-aside memories.

death is a trickster. it comes and goes
as morning turns to night turns to day
and we call it life until it isn't.

the old camera watched my childhood
leapfrog. I grew up too soon, learned
about dying before living

and your too-short journey left us lost,
looking behind doors, behind trees,
playing hide-and-seek that never ended

so I tucked away small treasures—
your blue stone earrings, a sliver
of granite scraped from your tombstone.

still I wait
until my heart gets finished
missing you.

For Aylan*

No, I'm thinking about leaves, falling and fallen. . .
      the red ones seem especially bright this year, spread
      good will like tainted wine, sing
      autumn's scratched-up
      sleep, grounded in our smuggy world.
      Leaves understand
      nature's shaking loose the sun's shoulder.

I hope you weren't thinking about the child
      face down on the beach, blue
      shorts, red shirt, worn three years,
      not even faded, still
      have life in them.

Take them to the Goodwill.
      also the little sneakers.

*Aylan, Syrian refugee whose body washed up on a beach in Turkey, September 2015

When the Video Runs on Fast Forward

I saw a video
watched a mother run
into a burning building
not once, not twice, but three times
to rescue her kittens.
She placed them one-by-one
on the street at the fireman's feet.
Singed fur, blistered face
anesthetized by raging instinct
a moment before her mothering ended.

Years and a mother's tears flow
into the life-stream,
grief and joy together,
a cosmic couple,
today wrapped in sunshine,
tomorrow vanished down-river
caught unaware in tangled birth-
days and collapsed sand castles.

Sometimes Guests Overstay Their Welcome

I.
You slammed the door shut so many years
ago when your Mama died, yet pain walks
back in, slips through the gashes in your heart,
the family you were born to, splintered,
never grew old, offers no solace.
II.
Don't ask pain to leave. It won't.
Make friends with it, invite it in.
Serve wine.
III.
Maybe then stories will sit down with you,
the one about Mama on Sunday mornings,
late for church again, how her young hands
smoothed the wrinkles in your dress. Daddy
waited in the car, lit another cigarette,
your shoes still untied.
IV.
And summer at the beach when you were five,
fried chicken piled in a Pyrex dish, flies buzzing,
waves wrapped your ankles, sparkling jewels
you could wear forever.
V.
Years rolled one on top the other, stacked
like quilts in the cedar chest. Her tiny porcelain
teacups refused to share their memories.
You can speak about her normal now, sometimes,
the snake uncoiled from your throat.
VI.
You smile for a moment, sense it may be time
for pain to leave, yet the visit hangs heavy.
Instead, you stand and pour more wine.

After the Singing

Just yesterday i heard my country sing.
the street jangled coins dropped
into tin cups, a brick mural wore
the hijab's promise and someone
i didn't know tossed me a smile.

jagged left coast, beaches bottom right
morph now into an inkblot drip, drip, drip-
ping off the map. words sink back
in my throat like downtrodden faces,
voiceless leftovers from a feast.

in the darkness, a baby hoot owl
caught in a trap moans
like the cold that settles
around stooped shoulders
about three weeks after the funeral.

II.

Women, if the soul of the nation is to be saved, I believe you must become its soul.
—Coretta Scott King

Sunday Church on the Deck

sun bosses everything today,
green hydrangea leaves bow low
next to grass wearing brown patches,
making a map of the yard.

thirsty immigrants sit at the
hummingbird feeder, not knowing
if they're welcome, not knowing
if they're safe.

Of course we have plenty
Mom always said
as she stirred up another
batch of Sunday rolls.

I listened to the trill
of the come-here birds,
a *thank you* for nectar
to savor along the journey ahead.

soon hummingbirds' wings
announced their return,
none the worse for wear
for having shared their table.

NYC Sidewalk

a scribbled note
tucked under

a shoe too
tattered to matter

against the frigid
blistery wind.

the note read
put me in a motel.

supplication
rooted me to the

moment,
pushed me

closer to the blanket—
threadbare

and there, on a shoulder

sat a raven, keeping
watch

so i turned
away, deathly afraid

of that bird.

Bad Things Happen When Roosters Crow and Dance

the slimy egg, salted and peppered,
slurs sideways on the plate as if to plead
"hold on to sanity." Then I see the sign,
whoever killed my hen may you rot in hell,
which is on everyone's minds these days. . .
hell
that is, and I had met Shakespeare the rooster
before, all ruffled red and cock-sure, watched
him prance and dance around the yard, circle
the girls, cluck how he loves them like they love
him,
just like the Donald proclaims insidious love
for his chattel, then adds oh-by-the-way
they must be punished
should their eggs get sucked into some
venomous void, and I watched him mount
the stage with bullets in his skull where eyes
should be, where the soul of Putin, we are told,
resides, and I sip from my coffee cup a rancid
taste of deceit, I drive by rough-hewn boards
splintered around the yard make-shift
marking the territory where the wall wasn't
built to keep the hen in whose tiny brain
and chicken feet walked right on down
to Mexico into the hot oil, stewed
into oblivion, a delicacy of chicken
bones just a few miles up the road
from hell.

FB Seduction in God-awful Times

the animal you see in the picture equals essence of your soul
the game declares.

i cry wolf
scoop up dead brain cells
killed by mindless activity
tripping over distractions, glad
i read 1984 back then when
it was filed in the fiction section.

how soon we forget o-say-can-you-see
what so proudly we sang heroes
crouched with ak 40-somethings lifted
on point, eyes rimmed in black because. . .?
i forget

but i remember grey helicopters hovering
above rice fields, thunk/thunk/thunking
the sound of beating hearts walled up
and i remember the dream, hear again
his wish for his 2 little children
& i see his 2 little children too
how they sparkled like tiny blue buttons
in november's sun.
i remember a storm in the desert sand
& another—easy to lose count.

& i remember how i once locked doors,
turned off lights, loved the warmth of you,
then fell gently away from evening.

now i stuff the scam of the day
into a couch cushion, slip-cover over,
remember to sleep with eyes wide open.

no consolation

from the ocean today.
it curls and throws kisses
before it turns under itself,
slaps at gulls then runs away.

i try to feel comfort here. the smiling
dog lopes toward me, her golden body
shakes dry in 4 seconds, releasing
fear and tension.

we don't see the wind, you know,
when it comes trampling, leaving
behind tattered sails, toppled trees,
a kite akimbo in a broken branch.

sun blisters. i shiver.
someone ensconced in luxury
presses a button for a brown butler
in a white house,
a child in a playroom
pushing around toy soldiers.

I Can Only Do Today

never before have I seen
tiny fingers curled
around cage wire
the child's eyes
a deep dark of fear
dragged across borders
by a mother's hands
folded in prayer

I helped a turtle today
seeking asylum in the pond
just a heavy shell
across its back
its tiny amygdala screaming
flee!
because fighting was out of the question.

Ugly Times

Hung a new fan on the outside porch today. Blades sliced the humidity, brought flutters of relief, but I coulda' sworn I heard a whisper, *Why bother? He's just gonna' start a war, you know, pack his suitcases full with green roots of evil, play golf on our graves.*

So I sat down with my new friends, squatters who swarm in my head now, crawl around uninvited, keep me awake every night. I tried to send them away, but they stay—then sunshine dropped its snarky self onto the grass as it has for eons, and just then in the oak tree, birds all lemony and apple red caught my eye. Audacious, I thought, while warships lecture each other somewhere, but I hear mothers still birth babies, brown babies, white babies, less than right babies, destined to be children (let us pray) but the rich bitch says now all must pay to play at school, lunch cancelled, so I wonder if I should get a refund on the fan, get a little money, a few dollars maybe, enough for a bottle of filtered water because a child I don't know drinks poison, or enough to fill your grandma's prescription, maybe enough to buy a wheel for someone's chair and then I remember those pussy hats waving from crowds, a sea of pink sails bobbing along almost like they were sewn together and all the feet moved as one river of blood.

I watched the fan circle. I coulda' sworn I saw a noose hanging on the oak tree out back
blackened against my scorched earth.

Pete

I never saw where he lived, but Daddy said he lived on the island.
I squealed when the siren blared and the drawbridge turned.
I thought maybe Pete was sitting in his car at the red light watching too as the sailboat slid through.

He drove up "on the yard" as the locals would say, paint-splattered pants,
suspenders over a t-shirt, thick, hard shoes.
Mama said, 'Hello Pete. It's a lovely day,' as he lifted forefinger and thumb
to his sweat-stained hat brim, eyes downcast.
Then he tipped his head towards me, a little girl of four.
He set his toolbox down in the grass.

I sat at the water's edge, watched how the men moved side by side, hammering,
lifting rough-hewn boards, constructing a rhythm of muscle, strength, trust.
Together, they built our cabin by the sea.
After that, I never saw Pete again.
But I've never forgotten the tall black man who tipped his hat to a child, ever so gently.

You never forget your shooting*

                        she said.

I'll never forget my first bicycle,
daddy's strong hands launching me,
only one scratched knee to tend,
and I remember evenings on the Bay,
shooting stars traced across heavenly
innocence where night birds frolicked
backlit by the moon.
I never imagined lilies
twisted away from sanity
one Easter kind of day as bodies
dropped into hallways.

Spoken by a survivor of VA Tech shooting on April 16, 2007

A Girl Story, circa 1960

We rode the same school bus,
but Trudy had boobies.
She sat alone like a scrub brush
by the roadside, her face pressed
to the window.
Some boy always dropped
down next to her like he was
doing her a favor.

One day, she didn't ride the bus,
her absence an exhale never missed.
Mom said she went to the *home*
out on the highway where girls went
who got themselves pregnant.

Christina in English class got all A's,
went to church, went all the way,
got herself pregnant, *shameful*
they said.
Her boyfriend marched in graduation,
then in Vietnam.

I saw a movie, sharp needles, dark
alleys, men jumping in & out of cars,
off & on girls with hollowed out
eye sockets, pain screamed,
life caught in a trap.

Back in my dorm I hung up my blouse.
Coat hangers jangled impatience
like little girls who just want
to go outside and play.

Women in the Shadows and the Secrets They Keep

her name
is Ashley
(Kavanaugh)

remember her
barbie face?
shallow eyes?

his accomplice
some might say

that would be
a cruel slap, though
her pain hidden
for all to see,
the shame she cries
into night's cover.

tell her instead
you are not alone

women choke
on their silenced
voices

scarred and tangled
they languish alone
in deep places

unless, until
they learn
to forgive
themselves

Judge Stepford*

'Something isn't right around the Court' Senator Whitehouse said staring at the woman holding a blank pad, posing for the future.

Was her law degree buried under her religion, forgotten like the First Amendment? Or was she thinking about people 'disappeared' from voting rolls or about mailboxes removed from sidewalks like extra chairs at the church supper?

I remember 1972 when something wasn't right in a town called Stepford. I cringed but kept turning pages, pictured women 'gliding through the local supermarket,' hair beautifully coiffed, smiles painted in garish red, brains in absentia. I felt the screams when they were disappeared and said 'thank you, Jesus, this is only fiction.'

And oh, how the whiteness of Stepford turned to darkness, misogyny turned to a wink and a nod, cruelty so entertaining, quaint, almost, like raising your right hand to take an oath you know you won't keep.

*The Stepford Wives by Ira Levin, 1972.

Who are the Dead

if not alive
somewhere else?
rustling leaves
down the street
and sailing above
treetops
with the nighthawk?

i believe the dead
roam,
restless
in the abyss
of nowhere,
visiting
the sick and sorrowful

and sit beside the child
never meant to sleep alone,
hugging a mylar blanket.

III.

*At the temple there is a poem called "Loss" carved in stone.
It has three words, but the poet has scratched them out.
You cannot read loss, only feel it.*
　　　—Arthur Golden, Memoirs of a Geisha

Divorce

it's not like stopping suddenly at a red light

it's easing onto the brake, tap, tap
then rolling through the yellow light

and it's not like locking yourself
outside in the cold, on purpose

you don't wake up one morning
and decide to burn the house down

it's more like a tree that gets worms
and dies slowly from within

or like the embers of a fire sending
sparks aloft that cease to be

like reading the last page of a book
you save to read again sometime

and that favorite tattered t-shirt, the one
you've always taken to the beach

also the baby pictures, the christmas wreath, cat's
grave in the backyard, neighbor's house key on the hook

and half-burnt candles on the mantel
you might light one more time.

Can a Day be Too Pretty

to be the day she dies, too sparkly, too vibrant with azaleas and sunshine? Still, it's time. I sit beside her and keep vigil. I touch her head, her soft fur. I speak quietly, say her name, offer water, food. She turns away, not unappreciative, but driven by instinct knowing she has no need to keep her failing body fueled anymore. Even so, she is beautiful, dignified, still haughty, so Siamese-y. But she's tired. She rests her chin over the lip of the cat bed. I tell her what fun she's been, I offer a taste of my cheese, but she doesn't climb into my lap and yell for her very own piece this time. Always a kick-ass spirit, her fiery attitude is what I'll miss most. She walked with aplomb, wore an impish smile just behind the mask. She settles into a calmness now, leaving me an unspoken example of a sweet life and memories of her tiny heart huge with love.

Exhale

forrest gump rain romps outside
slantwise as the poet advised

mounds of waves gather
like snowdrifts—or friends
coming to visit who change
their minds, turn away

still when nature shows off
the heart slows

quiet sighs into the moment
settles among sand dunes,
hums along with the windy chorus,
suggests I do the same

She watered her flowers in the morning

before the brutal sun had its way,
before our household stirred to hear
neighbors scream at their children
inside summer's open windows.

my stepmom tended her flowers lovingly,
snipped stems of pink azaleas leaving white
hydrangeas for all to enjoy, all the while
worrying about the children next door.

hers was not a garden, mind you, all trimmed-up
by rock walls—she liked free-range flowers
with spaces to spread straight or crooked around a tree
and that's how she finished the raising of me,

letting me grow wild near untended weeds,
always near blooms atop damp soil, basking
in the sun's warmth.

My Tree

The northeast wind off the Chesapeake Bay wanders among the fallen tree's dead branches, browses along like a museum visitor.

I am the single mourner at my tree's demise.

I lie in the grass, gaze up, see my tree's younger self, its splendid spire shading the fish-cleaning bench below where laughing gulls gathered on summer days.

I notice rusty hooks where the hammock once hung, once rocked my mother and me, and that branch on the other side, low-hanging, may have gone unnoticed had it not been the perfect size for tinkling wind chimes, had it not loved the beauty of quiet song.

Marsha Owens is a retired teacher who lives and writes in Richmond, VA, and at times, along the banks of the beautiful Chesapeake Bay. Her essays and poetry have appeared in both print and online publications including *The Sun, Huffington Post, Wild Word Anthology, Dead Mule School,* and *Streetlight Anthology.* She is a co-editor of the poetry anthology, *Lingering in the Margins.*

www.ingramcontent.com/pod-product-compliance
Lightning Source LLC
LaVergne TN
LVHW041508070426
835507LV00012B/1414